Contents

Be Your Own
STRESS BUSTER

A Roadmap to Meaningful Living

VISHAL BHANTI

INDIA • SINGAPORE • MALAYSIA

ISBN 979-8-89233-444-0

What Type of Life Do We Want?

Please take a moment to look at the pictures below and consider your reaction before starting to read this book.

Picture 1

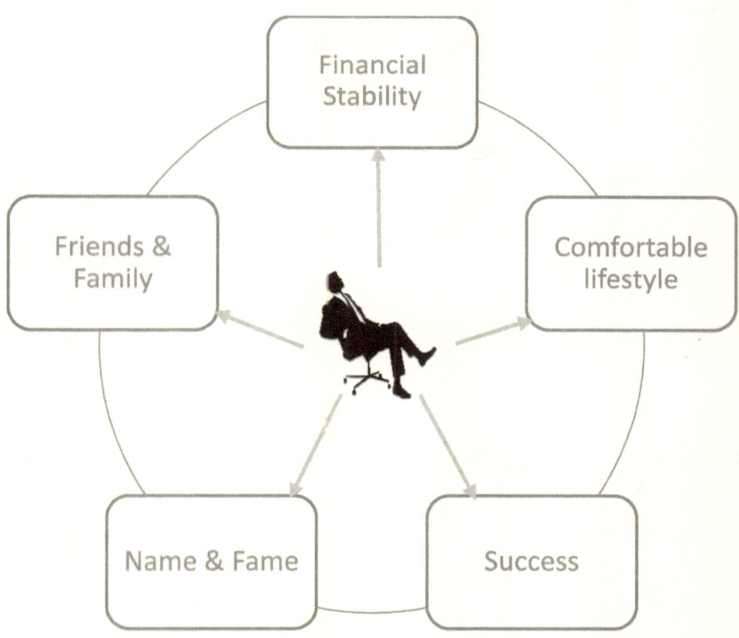

You adhere to the results-oriented methodology and concentrate on achieving your goals by following your success path. You strive hard to accomplish all of the above-boxed items because you believe you deserve them.

The direction of the arrows in this scenario indicates a desire to reach the boxed items.

Picture 2

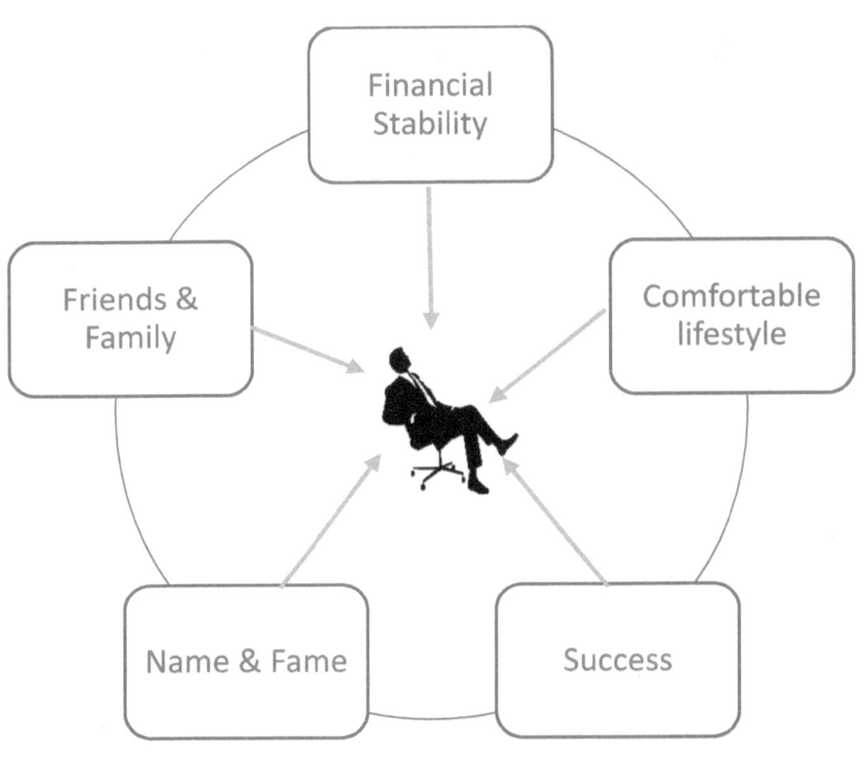

You put a lot of effort into focusing on and achieving your goals; you don't wish to acquire every item in the above box; instead, these accomplishments are a byproduct of your goal-oriented behaviors and are a part of your journey.

The arrows in this scenario point inward, are connected to personal objectives, and indicate that the things in the boxes are automatically accomplished as life is being transformed.

I hope you have selected your response. Both of the options reflect the trajectory of your life's growth and are realistic. It's possible that various groups will have different responses. Each will present arguments supporting the course of action they have taken.

Advocates of option 1 might argue that in order to get what we deserve, we need to be clear about what we want out of life and focus on taking a results-oriented approach. It is simple to traverse if you focus on results.

Supporters of option 2, however, will make different claims. Some may argue that one should enjoy the process of achieving their goals and make themselves so deserving that these necessary components will naturally flow towards them rather than focusing only on the outcomes.

Both are correct in their own ways; one's preferred way of living is up to them.

Now, let us look at a few more pictures.

Picture 3

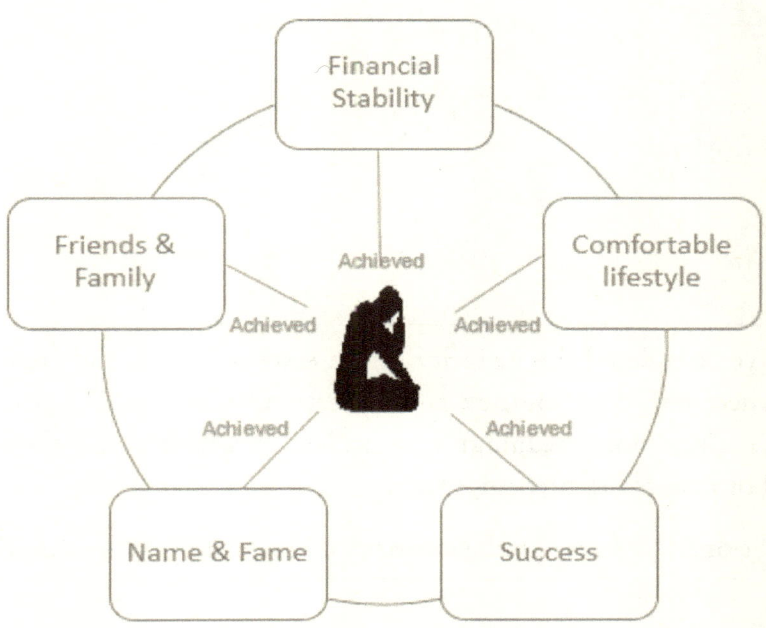

Regardless of whether you take a goal or results oriented approach, you consistently try to prove your relevance, however, you feel a sort of continual pressure in your life.

Picture 4

You've completed the majority of the essential tasks, and are quite satisfied with your journey, and understand how to make yourself and society more meaningful, regardless of whether you choose a goal or results oriented approach.

Additionally, you enjoy the journey and feel happy with your life.

Now stop and go back to pictures 1 and 2. Each of these approaches has benefits and drawbacks, even though it is ultimately up to the individual to choose how they want to live. When you want to standardize your life and find a long-term solution, the goal-oriented approach can be useful. Conversely, a results-oriented approach can be trusted for short-term, emergency and expedient working methods.

For instance, any government that formulates policies for its citizens takes a goal-oriented approach and makes sure the policies are sustainable and beneficial to the nation. However, in the case of COVID-19, vaccine development was an urgent matter that required immediate attention to save lives. Consequently, at that time, a result-oriented strategy proved more successful than a long-term goal-oriented one.

We now understand the difference between these two approaches, however, we'll observe how these different strategies impact our inner awareness and generate varying degrees of pressure and stress. However, once we are able to get rid of these stress-inducing habits and make **meaningful** life changes, our life will be prepared to offer us everything we deserve.

One thing is certain, though, no matter which option you select from pictures 1 and 2 you will, in the end, always choose picture 4. It is clear that, despite our desire for all the comforts, our ultimate objective is to experience true happiness and joyful moments.

Do you not think that we rarely have time for celebrations in this hectic world of ours? We rely far more on the outside world to give us these kinds of encouraging moments. To commemorate our happy occasions, we frequently wait for holidays, finals of football or cricket, quick getaways with friends, birthdays, anniversaries, and marriages. All the aforementioned scenarios have one thing in common, we all enjoy spending time with our loved ones. We still require an occasion, though, to enjoy our small circle.

One thing to keep in mind is that no matter what happens, you won't be able to celebrate the wonderful times if you are unhappy or under pressure from your struggles. We can state with confidence that our feelings of happiness or sadness are a result of both internal and external factors.

Emotional intelligence is the reason behind both feelings. This intelligence component, which varies from person to person, is crucial in determining whether we experience intense happiness or depressive symptoms.

These feelings are the basic forces that propel our intellect. Therefore, emotional presence is not our weakness. It is our power; these feelings allow us to live a fulfilling life and distinguish between happiness and sadness. Happiness may have different meanings for different people, and it is up to us to define our own emotional trajectories.

But in reality, most of us are struggling emotionally, which puts us more in line with Picture 3. Despite working hard, many of us struggle with stress, anxiety, and sleep disorders, that prevent us from achieving what we deserve.

We will embark on a journey to move from picture 3 to picture 4 in this book. Although it is a difficult change that calls for a strong commitment, I can guarantee that your life will be completely transformed if you use the techniques, that we will be going to discuss later in the book.

We'll now talk about the main issues in our lives in the upcoming chapters, along with some valuable frameworks and success strategies that can help bring about this change. As this book's title suggests, you need to be your own life's driver to resolve your issues, and it also depends on how dedicated you are to reaching your transformational objectives.

Emotional Intelligence Test

I would recommend first giving this quick test and getting your emotional intelligence qualities before you read further.

This test is a choice-based test that requires you to choose one statement in each pair of statements that describes you best. For each pair of statements, select the statement that best applies to you. Do not over-analyses the questions or try to think of "exceptions to the rule." Be spontaneous and choose the statement that comes closest to the way you are.

Occasionally there will be questions that ask you to make a close call between two choices. This is because the test is trying to distinguish between specific areas. If a question is very close and you can't decide which statement applies to you best, you can come back to it after you have completed the other questions.

Q1 – I am generally driven by?
A1 – My goals and objectives.
A2 – My family obligations and priorities.

Q2 – When do you feel happier?
A1 – When you buy your favourite and precious things.
A2 – When you buy a precious gift for your loved one

Q3 – How do you respond to a stressful scenario?
A1 – Able to response at your own and don't discuss much while facing these challenges.
A2 – Feel tremendous pressure but stay positive because of your confidence in your trusted group (Family, friends, mentor etc)

Q4 – How do you feel, when you realize that situation is not under your control?

A1 – You take on all the suffering and figure out some workable answers on your own.

A2 – Discuss issues with your inner circle and seek their guidance to identify a suitable resolution.

Q5 – Your risk-taking capability is based on?

A1 – Your own calculative approach, keeping your ultimate goals in mind

A2 – You take advice from a trusted group but final decision is always yours.

Now read the table below to find your emotional intelligence qualities based on your answers

If you have answered more A1	If you have answered more A2
You have better self-control	You are more empathetic
You have emotional creativity and you don't want any interference from others	You believe more on your trusted groups.
A sense of unaffectedness	You're always optimistic
You feel motivated	You find ways to get motivated

I hope this test would have helped give you a glimpse of your inner self.

This emotional intelligence determines the level of pressure or stress that a person can withstand, as I mentioned in the previous chapter.

If you go over the aforementioned questions once more, you'll see that these are real-life scenarios that we frequently face when trying to make decisions and in these kinds of situations, we sometimes lose our courage and refuse to deal with these unpleasant circumstances.

So, what does it mean and what is the advantage of giving the above test?

This test is being administered in order to make the realization that, in the end, our inner conscious mind always seeks solutions; when it is unable to come up with a plan of action, it behaves differently and occasionally loses its equilibrium.

We occasionally tend to lose our conscious courage and feel helpless due to a variety of internal and external factors. I think we've all encountered these unpleasant circumstances in our lives, and each of us has a unique inner strength for handling pressure.

An interesting fact that we can recover our emotional intelligence at any stage of life and get stronger to deal with these difficult circumstances is an intriguing concept. Understanding why we encounter these unpleasant circumstances and how they relate to the things we do on a daily basis is also crucial.

However, it would be beneficial to learn more about pressure, stress, and work-life balance before delving deeply into understanding the framework of our lives. We must comrehend the causes of stress' excuriating pain and how these elements impact us.

Why is Stress So Painful?

As we start this amazing journey of self-discovery, we will first discuss the primary problem that we are currently facing.

Stress: Are you experiencing this discomfort as well and are you looking for a way out? There are many different kinds of guidance out there. For example, we have access to books with motivational stories, spiritual content that suggests meditation, motivational videos, and habit frameworks. But these are mostly based on an individual's mental process, and there's not a lot of content out there where you can assess yourself and make plans based on your values and beliefs.

Although I have also allowed myself some latitude in providing some simple references, keep in mind that these are based on general experiences and refer to publicly accessible facts and stories that aid in context understanding. However, this book will be more interactive, requiring you to evaluate yourself and adjust your plans in accordance with your convenience.

Now, let us return to our problem statement and, instead of addressing it theoretically, let us discuss it considering the available factual information.

We experience anxiety or tension whenever we encounter difficult circumstances that exceed our present potential. You won't physically appear any different, but on the inside, you'll be fighting desperately to stay the same. Our mental health status is the cause of all of this.

Additionally, when we are sucked into an uninteresting or undesired activity, we experience a kind of pressure. We experience pressure when we work hard for something we don't care about, but we are said to be passionate when we work hard for something we enjoy.

It has been established by science that our bodies contain a hormone called cortisol, which varies depending on the individual and determines our level of stress, anxiety, tension, or alertness. People can handle stress in different ways and at different levels. Individuals' ability to manage stress is also influenced by other variables, such as age, genetics, family history, physical and mental health, surroundings, social networks, and connections. We are still unable to define the severity of stress based on the characteristics listed above.

A first grader may become disinterested in school if they don't experience a welcoming environment. A student in the 12th grade, on the other hand, worries about the final board exams. Could you describe the level of stress in each scenario?

No, we are unable to verify how serious stress is. A student in the first grade may be more serious than one in the twelfth grade, or the other way around. Their ability to manage stress will also vary and be contingent upon their present state of mind. First-graders experience different kinds of pressure or stress because they are not as exposed to the outside world as teenagers are.

As we've previously covered, stress is a mental state, and kids are using the plethora of fast, cutting-edge technologies available to us in this day and age. Their developing minds are exposed to the real world when they use these technologies at such a young age, and they respond as soon as their minds are exposed to the outside world. They get happy signals when they receive a positive response. Repetition of negative responses creates situations that kids are unable to simulate with the outside world and hence this results in pressure and stubbornness.

Global public sources report that 48% of people on the planet struggle to fall asleep, 77% of people experience stress that negatively impacts their physical health, and 73% of people experience stress that negatively impacts their mental health.

Do you find yourself constantly bothered by any stress? Life is prepared to present you with new challenges as soon as you overcome them.

We should be grateful that we are not alone in the universe because everyone's life would be described as, "Why do I have so many challenges?" However, a more general question is: Why do we choose stressful paths in life, and why is it impossible for us to live happy, stress-free lives?

In order to respond to this question, let's first examine the reactivity mechanisms, that are accountable for generating stressful situations for us.

Two categories of response mechanisms significantly influence our daily existence.

- **Non-interactive stress reactivity**
- **Interactive stress reactivity**

<u>Non-interactive stress reactivity</u> – This is also known as NISR, as a result of our mental state, NISR elicits responses from our ingrained ideas and beliefs. This kind of reactivity is also significantly influenced by our biases. For instance, a member of the middle class may develop an elite phobia and decide they don't belong to the so-called elite class by refusing to go to any such events out of concern that they will be insulted. As a result, these people create a phenomenon in their minds. These people may experience internal pressure and worry over a hypothetical situation due to this phobia, even if no one responds negatively to their background or upbringing or makes offensive remarks.

We had encountered similar circumstances in our school days. Exam phobia is what we term it. We construct a NISR scenario in our minds out of a fear of failing, which causes anxiety to rise and mental accumulation.

We all encounter similar circumstances in our lives where our minds trigger alerts depending on our perceptions and biases from the outside and inside, causing us to experience varying degrees of mental tension.

<u>Interactive stress reactivity</u> – Stress is also frequently caused by ISR, which is the result of our mind responding to the outside world through our social interactions. Due to our interactions, we can perceive a multitude of scenarios in our subtle surroundings, which can lead to stress. For example, because of the negative interactive reactions to one another, marriage abuse is a common scenario in which both partners experience stress and anxiety to some extent.

We can cite numerous instances of this reaction in which we experience the gloomy effects of this negative energy. Additionally, when your energy and interactive frequency do not match those of your respondent, your conscious mind triggers an alarm and releases cortisol.

The question at hand is whether the aforementioned instances always contribute to negative reactivity and instill some degree of fear in our minds.

So, let's examine whether stress can also be beneficial.

Yes, of course, it can be both positive and negative.

It is a known truth that challenges are not always detrimental to our lives, and these are the real instructors who teach us a great deal through practical experiences.

Different people are capable of handling these challenges to varying degrees.

Although we have no right to judge someone else based on their abilities or capacities, it is certain that we can grow and change into better exceptional responders who can deal with obstacles more skillfully.

So how do we address these issues and find a solution to prevent ourselves from entering a terrifying, stressful situation?

Quick fixes always appeal to a lot of us. Fast fixes are crucial, and they often work as well. However, these are only band-aid fixes that provide you with a veneer to cover up your anxiety or stress. They are not long-term answers to the issues.

Although few people use sleeping pills for restful sleep, they function similarly to a pause in the hibernation process, causing a corresponding increase in tension and pressure upon waking up. Although it is not our goal to discuss the science underlying these mental states, however, ignoring the actual situations increases pressure and stress.

What are the sustainable and structural solutions to keep our minds healthy?

There is no denying that the best core solution is a combination of medication, meditation, and spiritual guidance. But in order to follow this extremely fulfilling path in life, people need the right direction and instruction. This represents the second phase of improving our lives; however, prior to that, we must comprehend who we are on a deep level and give careful thought to the reasons behind our difficult circumstances.

Below are the two questions that help us understand these situations –

1. **Can we solve the current challenge, and can we control the situation?**
2. **Do we have the confidence to evolve with the required capacity to handle the situation?**

Now let us understand the results based on the responses diagram –

Picture 5

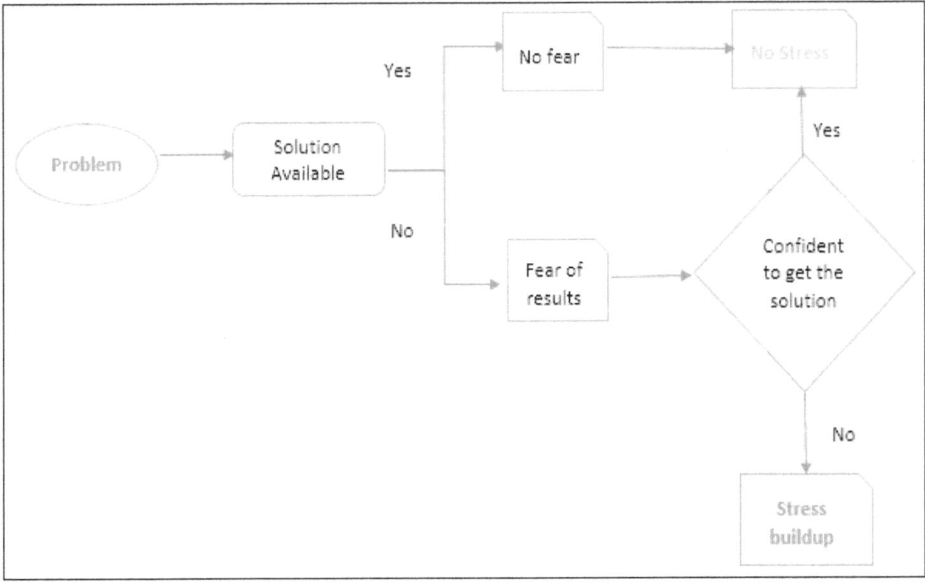

This is a simple response diagram; however, life is much more complex than this.

You would all agree that most of the time, we tend to find repetitive solutions to our different problems and become like a machine and thus get into the grip of tension, leading to depression.

I want to share one example of my close friend who lost his job in the last industrial slowdown, He was anxious since he had depleted his savings, and a significant amount of his loan's monthly instalments (EMIs) were supposed to be paid in the next couple of days. He was worried, as he could see the danger of losing everything because of being a defaulter.

It was good that he came to me and discussed his issue. We both tried to find the best solution, one option was to offer some money to help him repay his EMI, but this wouldn't solve the issue, as EMIs were recurring problems, but at least this could save him from his tension for a month.

The second option was to check the bank to see if they have policies to cover these few months' defaults. We also sought help from other close friends' circle so that they could help to find a job immediately.

First, due to this discussion, there was a relief on my friend's face to see that at least we could reduce the gravity of tension.

We executed all three options, and fortunately, he was covered in a policy that says that in case of a layoff, the insurance company would pay the EMIs for three months. Now my friend was slightly relaxed but had not fully recovered from his worry. We then circulated his CV to our network; it took time, but he got a decent job in the next four months.

The reason to share this example with you is to tell you that we need to decide and find an approach based on the situation. It is good to solve the problem on our own and bear the pressure but when it is not in our control, it is better to reach out to your inner trusted circle.

Sometimes, you won't get the complete solution, but at least a way forward can show you some light of optimization. Hence there are 5 key steps that we can take if we tend to see no solutions to our problems –

1. Communication with close and trusted groups
2. Reach out to the source of the problems to get some alternative solutions.
3. Be calm and think about what we can control
4. Work on core life principles to find permanent solutions.
5. Get learnings from our previous challenges.

There are also many researches done to get the age groups that are feeling continuous patterns of stressful environments and per the information available in the public, it says that stress burns are faced by **73% of people aged 30 to 60.**

Do we know what is the reason behind this and why this age group is more exposed to the world of anxiety and stress?

The most obvious reason is their work profile, and as this age group spends most of their time at work, they balance their whole life with work. Thus, a word has been invented to make us more worried; that is called **WORK-LIFE BALANCE.**

Many of you may not agree with the above statement because this is the only way in your current life to sync between your personal and professional life. But think again, what about the rest of the 27 % of people who are also in the age group of 30-60 but able to manage their stress successfully and don't build up unnecessary pressures?

Therefore, we can say that their stress-handling capabilities and managing their energies are better than the other group of 73 % of people.

So how to handle stress reactivity. It is challenging, we must know ourselves, our character, personality, core principles, and values. Each person is different and has their definition of good or bad. Hence, it is essential to know the self.

Moreover, we need to get out of the illusion of work-life balance and see how better we can manage our lives.

There is an elementary logic –

Life belongs to you, and your work is part of your life. Hence, work cannot drive your life. Having complete control over your life, work, or other activities would be the best way to manage yourself.

In this chapter, we understood the impact of a distressful life and how the whole world is suffering from stress reactivity, and I am sure that you will find a solution framework in the following chapters to manage your life and actions well and skillfully.

Delusion of Work-Life Balance

We often discuss work-life balance, but do you believe that there is a real-world equivalent of this term? This phrase implies that work and life are distinct from one another, but are they really? Work is only one aspect of life, life is a broad term. We should not contrast our entire lives with our work. I am not saying that you should not balance your life, however, must it be referred to as **LIFE BALANCE** only?

In developing countries, where people have very high expectations, a professional career has become very impactful in everyone's life. Such instances can be found in many nations, including China, India, Malaysia, Indonesia, and even a few developed ones.

Many of us think that we see the world through two separate lenses, one is focused on our work, and the other is kept personal and private. It's true in a sense but even though we wear different glasses, our eyes won't be any different. Life's balance problems arise from viewing the world through two distinct lenses.

We must discuss the circumstances from various points of view and according to how they affect our lives. While it is reasonable to divide our time between work and personal obligations, our fundamental beliefs cannot be altered. As a person, I am the only one who stays with my family and goes to work. So how could I be any different in the two situations?

The real issue arises when we begin to act in ways that are inconsistent with our basic beliefs while also trying to look like others. The pressure from the outside world causes us to lose our inner conscience, which serves as a bridge to our soul.

Anyone who is an introvert will be expected to interact with people more. The other guy will be asked to remain silent if he is the more outgoing one. However, why does this occur? because we give the outside world permission to dictate our feelings and behaviours.

The inclusion of the term "work" in this LIFE BALANCE is due to the widespread acceptance of the two lenses theory. Furthermore, we lose sight of our entire journey because we are so preoccupied with the tangible aspects of this professional world.

We may become confused and stray from our own goals and objectives as a result of these disparities in how we see life.

Let's use an example to better understand this. One of the goals of an aspiring organizational leader is to become the Chief Executive Officer (CEO) of an organization. He simultaneously desires a large, well-paying job to guarantee stability in his life. As he works toward his objectives, he receives an offer to join a company as a Chief Technical Officer (CTO) and receives the salary of his dreams. Since his materialistic needs are currently being satisfied, he stops working toward his objectives and becomes content and at ease in his surroundings. Although this person has accomplished the necessary results, he is still far from his goal.

Furthermore, results or outcomes are not inherently negative, rather, they serve as catalysts and facilitators for our progress. But living merely for the outcome would prevent us from reflecting on our own behaviour. When we only work hard to acquire a result and don't reflect on what we accomplish, we may lose touch with our inner selves. When we become honest and handle different aspects of life by evaluating our actions, rather than being reactive, we become proactive and can achieve a better life balance. We will discuss how we can enable these in the following few chapters.

Let's go back to our conversation on striking the correct balance between work and personal time. We all agreed, as we talked, that our personal and professional selves are not the same. Still, many would concur that they need to pretend and cover themselves under the lovely veneer of professionalism while they are at work. Ever wonder why this is the case? I'm still trying to find a solution.

In the modern realm of public relations, there are many areas where people are called professional when they get expertise in not telling you the facts but applying brain-hacking techniques to achieve the results they would like to see. Many of us are the victims of such brain hacking. However, as it involves a large amount of branding, sourcing, and authenticity, we must act on it sooner rather than later.

For example, Social media platforms use algorithms to analyze user data and curate content on individual feeds. The goal is to maximize engagement by showing content likely to capture attention. This constant stimulation and reinforcement contribute to addictive behaviour. You will progressively be exposed to any specific information once you become addicted, allowing you to lean toward any particular ideology.

The aforementioned example relates to our life balance issues. because it illustrates how we can enter the first stage of life balance issues when we lose our ability to make our own decisions and accept as true whatever the outside world says. Please realize that you are not always required to pay attention to external factors. But first, we must reflect on our actions and take appropriate measures.

Now let's see what happens when we only concentrate on the results expected from us, let's understand this with an example – Assume you work for a credit card company and are tasked with selling 100 cards in a single day. The sales team has set these goals in order to increase net profit by 10%. In this instance, what will happen? You might miss out on important family calls, lunch, and quality time with your children in the process of working tirelessly to sell 100 cards.

Is food only part of your personal life? Do your kids only talk when you come home, and they can't bother you while you are at work?

The issue arises from our distinct perspectives and reactive mindset, many begin after day five and then become terrified upon seeing the mountain. What choices do we then have? Let's say you monitor your progress towards the goals you have set for yourself regularly by assessing your actions. You can undoubtedly produce even better outcomes in that situation. This continuous performance tracker has been adopted by many new culture organizations, but there is still much work to be done in this area. Daily self-evaluation gives us several avenues to pursue in order to demonstrate improved outcomes. In order to accomplish the goals in this credit card example, the business could make use of contemporary technologies or undertake some open innovations.

Many of you would contend that if you are taking on a leadership role, you cannot reduce your work pressure, but this is untrue, I assure you. We all act in this way out of a sense of responsibility, but why is it limited to you alone? We also must ensure that, in our absence, someone behaves similarly to us. There may be certain circumstances in which you are required to be present and things cannot wait, in such cases, seize the opportunity without fail. However, don't restrict this behaviour to your professional life, why can't you apply the same moral principles to your personal life as well?

Let's now try to define the actual life balance. Take a two-minute look at the figure below and consider which smaller circles you prioritize or tend to the most.

Picture 6

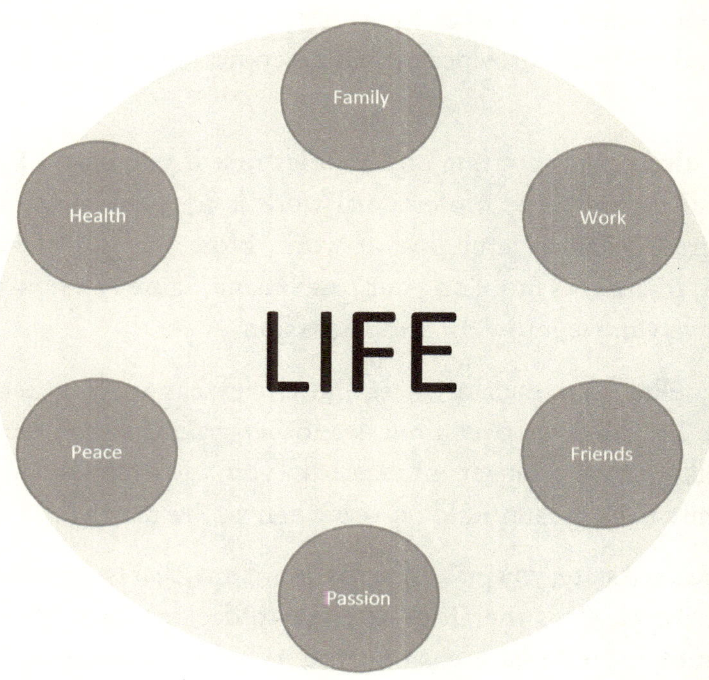

We'll arrive at this image shortly, but first, I'd like to share one example.

One of my friends had a great enthusiasm for photography, which was one of his great interests. He works as a professional banker, though, so he rarely has time for his passion. Every time I spoke with him, he would get a little irritated and swear about life at his office and like to escape to a quiet place to reflect on his passion. We had a great conversation, and at random, I asked him two questions:

Q: Do you enjoy your work?

A: He replied that it provides me with income, and that money is a vital necessity in my life because he wants to settle down and pursue many other goals.

Q: Do you enjoy your passion more than your work?

A: He replied that he is unsure but that he wants to learn more about photography. My job provides me with income, but photography is my hobby.

I would advise concentrating on liabilities first if you have a larger list of obligations and your professional work is not your passion. Keep up the great work in your line of work. However, if you have few liabilities, then focus more on your passion and figure out how you can progressively move into your area of passion.

Understanding that each of these life circles has varying degrees of influence on our lives over time is another crucial component. Your friends likely have a bigger influence on you when you're single, but your family has a greater hold on you when you're married.

In your relaxed state, you prioritize passion. Thus, that is the progression of our life cycle. It is therefore up to us to decide which life circle to concentrate on, and that focus needs to be in line with our obligations and liabilities.

Many people devote their entire attention to their work, which is what matters most to them. Additionally, it is a matter of balance in their lives, if they are deeply passionate about what they do, there is no harm in focusing solely on their work. It is therefore up to us to decide what kind of life we want.

Now let's go back to the picture 6, one thing is evident, striking the best possible balance between your life and circumstances does not entail allocating the same amount of time to each circle. Assuming that these circles are in a chord and you have total control over running this powerful chord of your life, hence, you can determine your path to nourishing them by estimating your capacity.

Many would argue that although they would like to implement a healthy life balance mechanism to instill values in their lives, their plans always seem to backfire when they face pressure from another aspect of their lives. It's true, but there are tools to evaluate your situations and actions. We cannot change the problem, but we can bring that change to ourselves.

We'll talk now about how our personalities and characters give us life balance and stress-free life, and we'll look into the frameworks that help us assess our behaviour. Additionally, we will witness a unique rules and challenge instruments for self-improvement, so I recommend reading the next few chapters.

Paradigm Shift at the Individual Level

We see people hurrying and not paying attention to traffic laws when we are driving on a busy street. What would you imagine to be thinking right away?

Many would argue that they are not part of the group and that the people who are breaking the law are not competent drivers. During the first few days, weeks, or months of the course, you will experience difficulties. After that, you may become accustomed to breaking the rules because other people are doing so.

This adjustment is an inductive chain reaction because the system will harass you indirectly if you don't adapt to that environment.

In this example, we change ourselves as a part of reactive mechanism and adapt to our environment. Since we don't have control over the actions of others.

Here, let's engage in reverse engineering. If you drive safely and in accordance with the law, you are preparing yourself for the circumstance and, instead of reacting to it, you initiate the change. It's a simple and much quicker natural process to change society once we begin to change within. Pt. Sri Ram Sharma Acharya is credited with saying, "I will change, and thus this society will change."

However, on the other hand, initiating a change in our own is difficult. This self-initiative necessitates a thorough understanding of our personalities and characters.

Let's now have a quick conversation about personality and character. Given how similar these two terms are, many people require clarification.

They are not equivalent, though. Characters discuss your innermost thoughts and principles, whereas personality describes your actions. Let's use a straightforward example to better grasp these two terms.

Let's say you are an introvert who shuns social interactions and stays away from these kinds of events. You think that going to these events would be extremely taxing. Since this example best captures how you behave when you socialize, it serves as a representation of your personality. It is also evident that although you are naturally introverted, you have a deep-seated kindness toward all people, are devoted to your partner, and are an honest worker. As such, these three virtues are integral to your inner essence and hence define your character in the same way.

Character and personality are complimentary traits that work together to improve you as a person. They are both equally significant. Understanding the resonance of your personality and character is essential.

You might think that when someone says they have "character," they mean personality, but that's not always the case. What distinguishes personality from character, and which one affects your general well-being more?

Our personality is the most important factor when considering who we are. It's everything that makes our identity and helps us decide our actions, passions, thoughts, convictions and life experiences.

Whereas your moral, ethical, and social attitudes and beliefs are reflected in your character.

Hence it is essential to know more about our own personality and character traits. This concept is known as the Personality and Character Quotient (PC QUOTIENT).

We will be going to discuss about the science of actions (KARMAS) in the upcoming chapter, along with how this personality and character framework can direct us toward making the right decisions.

For a quick reference. the quotient matrix along with a PC score can be found in the table below. (*Even though the personality and character traits will be explained in the upcoming chapter, keep in mind that this PC score computation is important to know now since it will be useful later on.*)

Occurrence Behavior	Character Positivity %	Personality Positivity %	PC Score	PC Quotient Status
In 60% of life scenarios, a positive and progressive attitude is demonstrated.	> 60	> 60	2	😊
Most of the time, you remain in a state of confusion and lack of focus on your ideas and behaviour	>30 & <60	>30 & <60	0	😐
Indicates a predominately depressed state.	<30	<30	-2	😔

#Since none feels good all the time, we have provided the percentage of the occurrence.

It could be argued that given their state of depression, their character positivity percentage should not be lower than that of those with a PC score of 2. Depression is not a sign of our character. Although this is true and in the above table, we are not defying the character, rather we are giving a percentage of positive attributes during the happy and depressed situations. let's clarify with an example.

An aspiring actor who works hard to land good lead roles in films, but at every audition, he is turned down. Eventually, he stops accepting his shortcomings and throws the blame for all of his rejections on the outside world. He gradually descends into melancholy and loses awareness of his subtle surroundings. Even though he has a good heart, the constant rejections have made him feel demotivated. The same person, who was eager to meet new people, is now not interested in hanging out with other people. He has had a significant psychological impact from these ongoing negative reactions, and it's likely that he will also lose the character's redeeming qualities. Having said that, not everyone responds to rejections in the same way, there are numerous encouraging tales of people who persevered in their hard work, maintained their emotional fortitude, and eventually achieved success.

Let's talk about a few more instances now to see how our personality is related to generating positivity and negativity, and how these vary depending on the circumstances.

Let's say you are an extrovert who enjoys attending parties and meeting fascinating people. You release tension and feel energized as a result. On the other hand, an introvert won't enjoy visiting these locations, and it would be unsettling to interact with the same astoundingly interesting people. Both personalities behave differently in the same situation, which causes their energy levels to fluctuate.

Let's now flip the roles, an introvert would prefer to move at a leisurely pace, along with their lovely thoughts, and without having to interact with others or the crowds. An extroverted person would not want to spend much time here and might experience anxiety when visiting these leisurely locations.

It is also a given fact that your personality will change over the course of your life. Compared to your older years, when you would be more at ease and serene, you would be livelier and more gregarious when you were younger.

It's fascinating to realize that all emotions, positive and negative, are equally important, as we've already discussed. There are lectures on optimism all over the world. With all the messages and quotes you come across every day, it's common knowledge that thinking positively is a good idea. These proverbs and sayings are encouraging and motivating, but they shouldn't be our only source of motivation. We need to look at the causes of the thoughts that come to us, both good and bad, and the importance of each.

We talked about cortisol, that is the hormone that warns our bodies of any serious dangers. Once more, let's attempt to comprehend this from a medical science perspective. Numerous hormones that are produced by our body are vital to our survival. Out of all these hormones, our mood swings are determined by two: cortisol and dopamine.

You feel good when you are engaged in any activity that makes you happy, enthusiastic, or appetizing. All of this occurs because your body releases dopamine as a result of this stimulating activity, which transforms your physical energy into the positive energy of your inner conscience and fosters more focused goals and positive solutions. Our morning walk is a simple example. While I'm not saying that everyone on the planet would enjoy going for a morning walk, many people find it to be a desirable and enjoyable activity to incorporate into their daily routine.

Let's examine the alternative situation. Nobody on earth wants to be in a position where they are being chastised. Your inner core experiences external pressure when you receive criticism from your supervisor, family, friends, or even strangers on occasion. This demotivates you. Your body creates more cortisol during this process, which functions as an early warning system for potential problems. The same thing occurs when you feel like speeding while operating a vehicle. These days, the technology alerts you with a beep, but your body also produces cortisol, which warns you to exercise caution to avoid an accident.

As a result, both happy and sad times serve as our alert systems. Consequently, the PC quotient table comes in handy when looking up your PC score. Periodic depression is perfectly normal, but in order to convert this cortisol into dopamine, you need to know when to slow down or speed up. We all understand that neither of the two circumstances is stable, which is why things in our lives are constantly changing. Our inner selves and brains will determine how we respond to these obstacles

A straightforward formula can be used to assess your character and personality and make sure you are headed on the right path.

"Act accordingly with how you would like to be treated."

Though straightforward, the aforementioned statement's eccentricity is incredibly important. Simply take a moment, consider this, and start by implementing it within your immediate family. Once a gradual shift occurs, you can observe whether it's improving your life in any way.

It is our mental state that determines how we act and react to other people. We can form an impressions matrix in our minds as we engage in numerous actions throughout our lives, which determines how those actions turn out.

In the upcoming chapters, we will go beyond stress management and will dig deep into the science of actions and Karmas as well as how this assessment techniques create a path for us to enhance the positive traits of our personalities and characters.

The Science Behind Our Actions

If you look at your own life, you will see that you do several things in a matter of seconds. Not all of your daily activities are instinctive and natural. For instance, breathing is a form of action that helps us survive. We take breathing for granted, but it's vital to our survival.

In addition to these simple acts, we take numerous other ones as we go through life. How many different kinds of actions have you handled since birth, if I were to pose a straightforward question to you? You'll reply, "We're not sure." An easy question with an easy response. ☺

The principle of action and reaction is well known to all of us. But it only explains the reasoning behind prompt reactions. Certain behaviours pay off over time and are explained by the science of Karma.

Let's start by asking a question. Who judges what behaviour is appropriate and inappropriate? Since every person has the right to their own definition of what constitutes good and evil, we are unable to accept any logic in this scientific world that is not tenable. There is no denying the veracity of this information. The good and bad aspects of your life are entirely up to you, as you are the master of your own actions.

Everything we say and do is stored in our inner conscience and leaves a lasting impression. The dynamism of the brain's white and grey matter has been studied extensively, and the results clearly show that these regions are responsible to our behaviour. There will always be two voices inside of you when you act.

Are we aware of how our inner core contributes to these conflict inputs?

Every action is always reviewed by our inner conscience. Whether or not we carry out the specific task is up to us.

Even though we are responsible for our actions, we are not entirely controlling the results, however, our actions may influence these results.

Fascinatingly, we control our actions, we control our corresponding impressions, however, we have no influence over their outcomes.

These perceptions provide outcomes predicated on your alert system. If you are a smoker, for instance, and you are aware that smoking is bad for your health, you are creating an impression. Whenever you go for a smoke, this impression will notify you; you can choose to ignore the alert or continue. Let's disregard your alert system now. The impression that is formed in your inner brain following each smoke will then accumulate your smoking habits and trend.

Throughout the course, this impression will be mapped to your physical condition. This impression will continue to bring you joy and pleasure when you smoke if your immunity is very high, however, as you age and your immunity begins to decline, this cumulative impression will alert you to danger. Alerts will be in the forms of warning signs of minor illness

The impression will further map your condition toward other consequences and may even give you a life-threatening alarm if you continue to ignore and carry out your smoking action.

In this case, it is evident right away that smoking is a bad habit. However, the effects of smoking can differ from person to person due to perceptions and correlations with one's physical state and circumstances.

Reading the aforementioned example helps us to understand that the logic behind this impression is an automated solution that is constantly present in our brains, recording everything we do and giving us results.

These various impressions are closely linked to our actions (Karmas). Based on these actions, we can categorize impressions into three categories,

- Indirect impressions
- Engraved impressions
- Intrinsic impressions

Now let's examine how these minds' impressions function.

Indirect impressions – Our indirect actions result in the generation of indirect impressions. For instance, you might participate in or carry out an action against your will because of outside influences.

Imagine an accident where the taxi you are riding in, hits a bike. Because you were not the cause of the bike rider's serious injuries, you, the cab passenger, decide not to report the incident. You rush and shut your eyes to that incident, starting to work on your task. Consequently, you will subconsciously develop a feeling in your conscience that you should have helped when you could have. It's definitely not your fault. However, nature still abides by the general service policy, so you may get this subtly negative impression.

Another example for you to consider is this: there is a marathon taking place in your community, but you are not interested in running. To make sure there are no erosions occurring, you consistently do plantations and water your plants as well as settle down the dust. Runners appear delighted that this track is dust-free and clean when a marathon passes through your neighbourhood. You won't realize it when you settle or clean up dust, but deep down you'll feel that it's beneficial for your surroundings as well as for me. A favorable indirect impression is an outcome.

Additionally, the outcomes of these indirect impressions are also indirect, and you won't know much about them.

Engraved impressions – These impressions are the outcome of deliberate actions that are being taken with specific goals in mind.

Because of these engraved impressions, results have a certain amount of set validity. These are similar to planned actions that yield outcomes predicated on the calculations of your present life.

Assume that your wish when getting a drink is to get wasted and enjoy yourself with your pals. Because you like it, you start doing this once a week. This habit will give you a result after a predetermined amount of time. Depending on your pre-existing favourable impressions, this effect may or may not be substantial. But either a fatty liver, a weakened immune system, or worse, a heart condition, will befall you.

However, if you become aware of your inner alert system and adjust your behavior accordingly, you will experience a significant improvement in your health and outlook. To achieve this, stop this habit, start leading a healthy lifestyle, and follow a suitable diet. That is the power of warning system of your engraved impressions.

You will find it fascinating to learn that the impression works on the basis of a straightforward mathematical accounting formula. Your past deeds and impressions also matter a lot in achieving the intended gravity of results. Since I am aware that this concept can be a little difficult to understand, let's look at an example to help.

A decent young man enters politics to serve his country and works hard to uplift his constituents. He participated in the election after engaging in this social activity for nearly 15 years but ultimately lost it due to a lack of funds. Still, he puts in a lot of effort and runs for office again the following election. He is afraid of losing the election because he does not have enough money to support his victory. However, his prior integrity has now paid off, as members of his constituency step up to offer their cash, labor, and moral support in order to ensure his victory. When he was finally elected, he was not given a position of authority that would have allowed him to implement appropriate policies. Nevertheless, he never gives up and keeps trying to do his best to support his constituents. Eventually, after everyone see how committed he is, the party leadership offers him a great position in the government where he can also set policies. Over time, he began to gather favorable impressions, and as a result, his luck began to turn to his advantage.

If we examine his journey in detail, it appears to be a moral tale about someone who is always trying hard to make a good impression, but this is very hard to follow. A very small percentage of people stick to their goals and don't stray from their main focus.

People experience feelings of discouragement and failure when they don't see results, but if you now begin to consider things from these impressions' perspective, you will see that everything is normal. Time will always change if you are moving forward positively and at a steady pace.

Intrinsic impressions – The impressions that result from our qualitative actions and provide us with longer-term or wider outcomes are known as intrinsic impressions. There is an intersecting logic to support the reasoning behind this type of impression, which yield results without distinct timelines.

Let us imagine that there is a man who has a strong desire to take his cousin's property and is unconcerned with morality or the law in the process.

In the end, he succeeds and takes ownership of this asset without legal authorization. This illegal activity will leave a lasting impression on his conscience. His soul's endurance and prior indelible impressions will determine these outcomes.

Now let's return to the example. This person currently enjoys his life and has arrogated the asset, successfully taking it to the next level. People may believe that he is growing rapidly in spite of his illicit and immoral activities.

How then does the impression law function?

It's actually working because there are currently no favorable circumstances for this horrible action to yield results.

Assume that he began with an asset worth ten million dollars, grew it, and earned a profit of one hundred million dollars. He might then experience a major setback in the future, but his outstanding work in the past has kept him in a time zone where his bad feelings are postponed, so the blow is not felt. Once the initial positive impressions have faded, his immoral actions will start to come back to haunt him. Moreover, it is commonly known that negative impressions start to come back when you are mentally and physically weak.

There are numerous ways to make up for a negative impression. He may encounter a dire financial crisis, become sick and have to spend his entire savings on medical bills or face legal issues. Anything that would bring him the same kind of severe mental trauma he had inflicted upon his cousin.

For the sake of another example, let's say that you visit a plantation drive once a week and there you have roped 100 plants. Your goal in doing this is purely altruistic, you don't anticipate receiving anything in return. That being said, this impression would still function organically and be intrinsic, not neutral. All these impressions will be noted in your positive account book, and the results will be computed. If participating in the plantation drive has brought you any immediate benefits, do let me know. But you'll notice that all along the way, you helped this lovely mother nature, came across a lot of nice people, and cleared out a fair amount of pollution. You will begin to feel better and somewhere this good impression will help you.

Now we understand the science behind our actions and how these actions create different type of impressions.

But there could also be opposing viewpoints. Being too cautious before acting is not beneficial. The world moves quickly these days, and we don't have time for our feelings. How then could someone analyze or plan their actions to such an extent? If we over compute every time, we will make decisions much more slowly and the universe as a whole will face a huge conundrum.

To succeed genuinely, you have to act. Your core beliefs and principles must be in line of these actions. There's no need to second-guess yourself before acting if these are exactly in line. That being said, in order to accomplish this, we must be aware of our guiding ideals. We therefore know that recognizing and appreciating our basic beliefs and principles facilitates the process of making good impressions. However, what exactly are those tenets, and how can we codify them? This is not an easy task. Values ought to be central to who you are; they shouldn't be ingrained in your culture or routine. A straightforward strategy to make a good impression is to act in accordance with your morals, ethics, and values. Your basic life values will never change, regardless of your upbringing, career or personal status, financial situation, success, or accomplishments.

The personality and character assessment framework is provided below, along with a few scenarios. I would like you to record your answers for each line item. This brief assessment will now help you to determine your PC score.

Core Values Area	Traits	An example scenario	Your Response
Personality	Conscientiousness	You consistently accept responsibility for your work and offer trustworthy solutions.	Yes or No
Personality	Agreeableness	It is more important to you to allow your children or subordinates to express their opinions than it is to try to control or dominate them.	Yes or No

Core Values Area	Traits	An example scenario	Your Response
Personality	Addictiveness	You are content with what you have, and it doesn't seem like any addictions are actually necessary for you to enjoy life.	Yes or No
Personality	Emotional Stability	Even though depression can happen to you sometimes, you can control it.	Yes or No
Personality	Assertiveness	You have the self-assurance to express yourself to others.	Yes or No
Personality	Resilience	You have the ability to quickly recover from setbacks and keep an optimistic approach on all issues.	Yes or No
Personality	Creativity	You've ability to think outside the box, generate original ideas, and approach problems in innovative ways.	Yes or No
Character	Honesty and collaborative vision	You are a person with vision, and you incorporate other people into your vision for overall growth.	Yes or No

Core Values Area	Traits	An example scenario	Your Response
Character	Compassion	Even though your outer mind is screaming, you remain composed and behave with basic human decency.	Yes or No
Character	Compassion	You experience inner joy and happiness when you lend a helping hand to others	Yes or No
Character	Compassion	You share others' joy as well as sadness	Yes or No
Character	Integrity	No matter what, money never attracts you to do any immoral tasks.	Yes or No
Character	selflessness	With your earnings, you donate to charitable causes without any personal gain in mind.	Yes or No
Character	selflessness	Your feelings are not driven by any self-serving goals or intentions.	Yes or No
Character	Social conscious leadership	Your goal goes beyond making money and focus to include improving society as a whole.	Yes or No

Core Values Area	Traits	An example scenario	Your Response
Character	Strategic open-mindedness	You are competitive, but you also value other people's abilities and knowledge and place more faith in your own abilities and hard work.	Yes or No
Character	Strategic open-mindedness	You employ rational thinking to outperform rivals and respect differences in viewpoints.	Yes or No
Your PC score would be +2 if you scored more than 4 YES on the personality assessment and 6 YES on the character assessment.			

This framework defines general human principles, it is not predicated on any moral policing, as one can observe. Different flavours may be influenced by your location, circumstances, surroundings, culture, and demographies.

For a simple example, think about this: a fruit vendor in a remote area of India will take different factors into account than a large-scale business magnate operating in the heart of Silicon Valley. Still, they may run their businesses with the same fundamental beliefs and core values regardless of the amount of money they make.

A fruit vendor will likewise adhere to the same principle and may consider splitting his earnings with farmers or consumers, however, a business magnate will consider his organization and the nation's economy as a whole. Using the money, he makes, he might also provide a better life to others. Hence, they both will make a good impression in these different situations because of their generally positive thought process.

Let me caution you here as well, even though it is obvious that we must try our hardest to leave a good impression. It's quite likely that you'll get caught up in the unfavourable aspect of favorable impressions. Encouragement of positive impressions can also show signs of diabetes; their sweetness can taint your morals.

A king's tale was found in old Indian texts. He went by the name Bharat and was well-known for his kindness and bravery. He was a magnificent monarch, and his realm grew to include every corner of the planet under his rule. The term Chakravarthy, which means "the one who had won this world," is found in Sanskrit. Thus, Bharat came to be known as Chakravarthy Bharat.

In his kingdom, everyone lived in such happiness and gave the king full credit for their good fortune. After realizing he had done a great job, Bharat decided one day that his name ought to be inscribed on the highest point on Earth. A saint he visited advised him to travel to the highest point on Earth, the Himalayas.

Himalaya's saint asked him to visit Lomash Rishi, another saint, as he was unaware of any such location. Being an immortal, Lomash Rishi was well-known. His running age was not calculated. At that point in time, he was the oldest man alive. Bharat followed the advice and requested Lomash Rishi to give him some time, asking for his kind advice on his sincere question. At last the day arrived when Bharat could finally meet this magnificent soul.

As Bharat was about to ask his question, he introduced himself as King Chakravarthy Bharat. But Lomash Rishi cut him off, inquiring as to how many Chakravarthy kings we were dealing with.

Bharat looked around in shock at first. Then he said, "Everyone already knows that I am the only person on this planet."

King Lomash Rishi said kindly, "I'm so sorry."

I have spent countless years on this planet, and when my lone hair fell out, it witnessed a whole generation during those millions of years. You can now determine my age because I've lost thirteen hairs. There is only one Chakravarthy king like you in a millennium, and because I am getting older, I think I am forgetting how many kings there are.

The statement has now been understood by Bharat. He acknowledged his error right away and expressed regret for his actions.

Has the core of the story escaped your notice? For all your sincerity, you should never take pride in the good that comes from your work; instead, you should be wary of the magical disruption of your good work. You therefore run the risk of receiving some negative impressions in addition to pure positive ones from your good deeds.

However, you ought to continue to relish your accomplishments and inspire others to achieve great things. It is our collective responsibility to take pleasure in the fruits of our optimism in a way that inspires others to act morally. Credits and recognition for our outstanding work will automatically occur; however, our soul's purpose is to accomplish the things we are meant to do, not to receive praise from others.

You will witness a great deal of people becoming involved in this entire journey, and they will also benefit from your success. As you continue toward your more ambitious objectives, let them enjoy.

Therefore, we must uphold our ethics and values in order to obtain the high level of satisfaction shown in Picture 4 in Chapter 1. To put it another way, according to PC Quotient, our PC score needs to be greater than 2.

In Sanskrit, there is a sentence –

"TAMSO MA JYOTIRGAMAYA"

Meaning: God, please help us to pass from the dark into the bright light of my life.

This statement is still frequently uttered in India, but it's more than just a saying—it's a practice of our life that encapsulates all of the aforementioned values. When we put these ideas into practice, the outcome is

"TAMSO MA JYOTIRGAMAYA"

Thus, we will discover in the upcoming chapters how to raise our PC score as well as how to draw strength from our fundamental ethics and values.

Five Rules Framework of a Successful Life

We covered the idea of Karmas (actions) and how to make a better impression in order to align with outcomes and success in our previous chapter.

Since it is very difficult for us to handle every action on a daily basis, we must create a set of rules that will enable us to choose the best course of action. These guidelines are derived from how the conscious mind functions within.

Everything we say or do leaves an imprint on our inner conscious mind, and this inner core shapes the context in which we think and behave throughout our lives. Controlling our thoughts and behaviors is simple if we can master our inner selves.

We talked about impressions, Karma, stress, and anxiety. Why do we need to create a good impression, why are we learning to manage our stress and our actions?

All of this is motivated by our desire to advance as people and live prosperous lives. (picture 4 of chapter 1)

I have created a framework of rules to assist you in learning some important success rules.

Rule 1 – Move on and extend forgiveness

Who hasn't suffered because of the words or deeds of another?

Our inner brain records a negative impression of the person who hurt us, and we harbor resentment towards them. We feel bad vibes whenever we see that person. We frequently mistakenly think that the negativity of that individual is the source of these negative vibrations, but in reality, it is our memories.

Our inner conscious mind creates a space where it builds a defense mechanism and stores negative energy to counteract any negative impression that we may have. Even if you happen to meet your crush in a very sultry and foul place, you will still feel a strong bond with them. Conversely, you are meeting someone in a seven-star luxurious place who you perceive to be sly and who constantly tries to impede your progress. Can you still enjoy these 7-star amenities? You will undoubtedly make an effort to leave this location as soon as possible.

Why is this the case, and in the two examples above, why are the surroundings the least significant? All of this is a result of our personal impressions, which are kept in our conscious mind or inner core. Therefore, letting go of these painful memories is essential.

What is forgiveness?

This entails making a conscious choice to release animosity and bitterness.

We release that person's perceptions and set them free when we let go of this anger. We must release them since we are the ones who gave them spaces in our innermost being. Forgiving someone might even make you feel sympathetic, empathic, and compassionate toward them.

We will feel lighter and be more able to conceive of positive ideas after we let go of these feelings. You won't harbor resentment toward them as a result, and you won't experience any bad energy. A few advantages of forgiving are listed below:

1. Better mental health
2. Positive thinking
3. Reduced likelihood of anxiety and sadness
4. Better self-esteem

<u>Rule 2 – Compete with self</u>

Nobody enjoys the difficulties and pressures of competition. However, it is not too difficult to comprehend that our own evolution has occurred because humans have been able to compete with other races and have emerged as the most powerful species on Earth.

We compete with people around us in the modern world. Employees compete with colleagues in the workplace and students compete with other students in the classroom; this is beneficial for improving our performance.

Let's now consider an inventor who created a tool or instrument that has aided in our progress. They challenged themselves and engaged more in competing with self.

Not only we do improve as better souls when we compete and challenge ourselves, but we also have the ability to create something useful for other people.

There are three major benefits of competing with self –

1. **Improved capabilities –** We don't establish boundaries when we compete with ourselves. Since there is no quantifiable goal, we constantly strive to outperform our previous performance. As a result, we constantly push ourselves and our boundaries.

2. **Clarity in order to succeed –** When we compete with ourselves, we stop considering other people as success benchmarks. It makes sense that you would be influenced by other people and inherit a great deal of things in life. However, when we compete against ourselves, we create our own success tales. We should not let other people set our expectations for us or act as our guide when defining our own success. When we act in this way, the delusion of success escapes us. No one else can obstruct your path to success if you are content and know exactly what needs to be done to meet your goals.

3. **Moving the benchmarks of victory** – when we compete with ourselves, we never sit back and enjoy our successes. Instead, we celebrate and spread joy among our loved ones, but we also never stop pushing forward and establishing new goals for ourselves. The reason it loops back to the beginning is that when we push ourselves beyond our comfort zones, we discover new limits, which feeds the cycle.

<u>Rule 3 – No to procrastination</u>

The act of putting off doing something until the very last minute and ignoring the consequences is known as procrastination. The main cause of the stress that accumulates in our lives is something that we all encounter or experience on a daily basis.

The first sign of losing focus is when your phone buzzes and displays your social media notifications while you are working intensely on office work. You begin to flick through your notifications and repeatedly launch mobile apps. Sometimes, even you forget that why you have opened your mobile. You try to focus on your work again and go back to your real life. This pattern of unwelcome distractions blurs our vision and impairs our ability to concentrate.

Procrastination has a plethora of modern content available. A lot of them advise us to schedule our daily tasks and to set deadlines for ourselves. To a certain extent, this is accurate since success is guaranteed when we operate according to real deadlines. But we also need to be aware of our priorities. Not everything we think or intend to do is crucial. We have to be aware of what is most important to us at the time.

There are many negative consequences of Procrastination

1. Lack of clarity in life.
2. Stress build-up and depression
3. Continuous anxiety.
4. Failures in life.

Distraction is the primary cause of procrastination, as we have discussed. Therefore, we would need to practice the habits that will improve our ability to focus. But aside from lack of concentration, there are a variety of other causes of procrastination:

1. You are unaware of the necessary actions.
2. Unable to choose what to prioritize.
3. A lack of enthusiasm for what you do.
4. A lack of self-control in accepting accountability.
5. Have a belief in pressure management strategies and wait to start your work until you are under a lot of pressure.
6. Poor mental and physical well-being.
7. Constantly await the ideal opportunity.

Procrastination only escalates as a problem when it starts to interfere with everyday life and becomes chronic. In these cases, ineffective time management is not only a problem for them; it's ingrained in their way of life. In our upcoming chapter, there will be several tasks that are intended to eliminate this particular behavioral shortcoming.

Rule 4 – Rejuvenate physical and mental energy

Let's examine the example below to better understand this rule:

A teenage boy who had all kinds of comforts in his life used to live with his parents. With lots of friends, he was attending a top-notch school. Though everything he needed was in his home, still his mind was looking elsewhere for something truly enjoyable. A strong desire to travel consumed him. He arranged a party at the neighboring shoreline one day with his pals. All the guys were having a great time at the beach, and the evening party was really great. The plans were going well. This boy had some heated arguments with his father that morning, that was why he was a little upset. Both the music and the food did not appeal to him.

The next day, he decided that he ought to visit a serene location to obtain some good energy, so he packed up everything he owned and headed for a hill station.

He was now encircled by a lake with blue water and in the middle of gorgeous hills. He was starting to feel at ease. He spent the entire day sitting still and admiring the magnificent scenery. He was happy because he had chosen to enter the lap of nature.

Now the dark night was rapping on the door of day. This young man was trying to fall asleep, but he was having trouble. He felt a little uneasy in these extremely dim surroundings now.

The same man, who had once found significance in two distinct places, was now experiencing anxiety and, in the end, desired to return home.

The moral of this story is that we have likes and dislikes in our minds, and if those thoughts are unresolved, they will force us to be their slaves, acting on the advice of our unresolved thoughts. Controlling our thoughts is therefore crucial.

There are numerous methods that can assist us in achieving mental stability and serenity. It is obvious that as we get older, our minds change and behave differently, but if we instill a method in our kids at a young age, they will be equipped to face life's challenges as they get older. The methods listed below are used to revitalize our mental and physical energies:

1. Daily exercise
2. Mindfulness
3. Meditation
4. Practicing of YOGA.

Rule 5 – Sync with Nature

All living things are composed of the five fundamental elements—water, sand, air, fire, and space—as proven by science. It is never easy for us to live when we notice deficiencies in any of these five elements, either in our physical selves or in the outside world. Is there any way you can live without any of these five things?

Spirituality, which goes beyond merely worshiping or praising the divine, is something that people in India believe in. Being spiritual is nothing but to have real connect with nature and go within oneself.

The image of Lord Shiva is a true illustration of how people have interacted with nature for eons.

Picture 7

His appearance represents five fundamental elements and is actually a representation of the power of nature.

- Lord Shiva's body is always covered in ashes, which stand for EARTH, or sand, the first element.
- TEJAS, a bright light behind his face that resembles the second basic element FIRE, is what gives him a charismatic aura.

- On his head, there is a half-moon that resembles the letters SKY or SPACE.
- A stream of water appears to be coming from his head; this represents the fourth element, WATER, and is reminiscent of the sacred Ganga river.
- We can see his DRUM and TRISHUL on his right. A drum creates or generates a buzz in the atmosphere. Thus, the fifth element of life—air—has a significance akin to a drum.

I brought up this illustration because spiritual teachings also teach us to worship the almighty, who has the ability to control them and resembles this nature. With his immense power, Lord Shiva can create or destroy life. With the help of these five fundamental components, he accomplishes this. Therefore, worshiping Lord Shiva in India is really a form of worshiping mother nature. Similar to Shiva, we can also be pure and enhance our lives by harmonizing with these elements of nature.

Undoubtedly, developing spirituality requires devotion, and if we believe in the existence of a higher power, we also need to have faith. The manifestation of Lord Shiva is further evidence for this idea. A dead body is referred to as a "SHAVA" in Hindi. When we are unable to breathe, we are considered dead. As a result, we lose AIR, the first fundamental element. Our bodies begin to deteriorate and our organs stop functioning the moment we are removed from oxygen. As a result, our physical existence ends. Finally, we reach the actual soil.

However, a living thing possesses the ability to revive this lovely existence. This is made possible by the five factors listed above.

You will also notice how these five elements are present in the lives of birds and other animals. Because of our habits and addictions, we humans are unable to connect with the central chord of nature, despite having similar or even superior senses to perceive this resonance.

Let's examine how birds and animals interact with the natural world. Every living thing on the earth uses wisdom and senses to overcome obstacles in life. They are constantly led or alerted to stay on the correct path by these senses. Have you ever witnessed a tiger munching on grass or a goat devouring red meat? Even though they lack the education that humans possess, these animals never come into contact with food that is inedible to them. They can identify because they have acquired a taste and an understanding of what is appropriate or inappropriate for their physical needs over time. Therefore, the tongue serves as our first line of defense, warning us before allowing any food inside.

As humans, we also taste a wide variety of foods, but we prefer to taste foods that are edible and flavorful. It doesn't follow that the tongue forbids us from consuming any harmful foods. Our tongue warns us not to eat too much when we consume red chilies. This also applies to other harmful substances, such as alcohol, cigarettes, junk food, etc. When we consume these harmful substances, we are alerted, but if we ignore it, we will go against the natural order and become out of balance.

Moreover, diseases arise from this. The severity of illnesses is determined by the impression of maturity left by our actions, as we covered in our previous chapter on Karma. But there's no denying that consuming anything poisonous will undoubtedly be bad for your health.

Therefore, any action in harmony with our senses' alerts is also harmonious with nature. Like the tongue, our senses of smell, hearing, and sight help us choose the appropriate items for ourselves. Whether or not we follow the path, these senses always indicate us to be on the right side.

Mother Nature is a merciful force that guards us against evil and punishes us when we disobey her laws. These guidelines are defined by our own senses and, as we have already discussed, are not found in any books. However, there's one fundamental law of nature: whatever you take, you have to give back to keep it unexploited. It is also arguable that we are unable to restore nature to its entirety. Although we can't make coal and give back to nature. In this instance, the benefit would be seen by planting trees and research into other energy sources to minimize the need for coal.

We can each exert ourselves to the best of our abilities as individuals. It is not necessary for us to wait for others to initiate the changes. A villager who also farms can make sure that the soil is not getting worse and can take steps to improve its quality. Urban workers may want to consider lowering their carbon footprints. Cleaning up the environment is something a society can consider. Individually, we can promise not to contaminate our water sources (oceans, rivers, and canals).

Since we humans are extremely familiar with these concepts, we don't need any advanced degrees to assist the natural world. In our lives, we must carry out these little tasks. You will witness and sense mother nature's love, which is unchanging and pure even though you are only exerting little efforts.

The five rules listed above will help you understand your basic human values and beliefs, which will improve your personality's and character's traits. Furthermore, even during your most trying period, there is no possibility of trouble if you are on the right path.

But here's the thing: while everyone is aware of these guidelines, we hardly ever see them applied in real life. We always make an effort to abide by them, but sometimes, because of our own prejudices, circumstances, and conflicts, we fail to do so and choose a course of action that keeps us apart from our inner selves. We'll talk about the Six Challenges Framework in the upcoming chapter, which could help you practice your values more organically and get closer to your soul.

Six-Point Challenges to Reinvent Yourself

In the previous chapter, we covered guidelines for leading a happy life. But you have to practice them if you want to reach this level of perfection.

We should all consider how to attain this regularity. Understanding ourselves is the first step towards developing this positive trait, if necessary, we may need to create a new version of ourselves.

That is why this chapter is devoted to the topic of reinventing ourselves.

Let us first discuss, why did I keep the title of this chapter "Six-point challenges to reinvent yourself". Why, though, is it a challenge? Being responsible for our actions, we have the freedom to choose whether to take positive or negative actions.

Will you find it easy to give up tobacco if you have an addiction to it? No, is the response. Everything we do has turned into a habit and a never-ending cycle of obsessions.

Let's look at one more illustration. Your inner self will alert you when you go for a smoke because you want to stop, and if you can't break the pattern, you'll continue to smoke with the thought that you'll stop next week, month, or year. A whopping 99% of people don't follow through on their resolutions. We all enjoy and feel proud that we had made some resolutions, but we could not even stand for two days. These are the new, funny jokes.

Tell me now, is it easy to reinvent yourself or is it very difficult to become a better version of yourself? Voting for the latter option is what I would do. There was a rope and pulley system back in the old days when people would go to the well to get buckets of water. There were large notches everywhere because this rope was constantly being roughed up by the well's edge. Can these marks be removed this quickly? In order to undertake some renovations, thorough maintenance and work are required.

Our lives are no different in this regard. We become so accustomed to a certain way of life that we are unable to start such changes even when someone suggests it. It requires a comprehensive overhaul of your inner and outer core. For this reason, we are calling these changes as challenges.

If you can finish these six challenges, you'll be a different 2.0 version of yourself. As we discussed in the previous chapters, the PC score and the Five Rules framework assist you in making the right decisions. However, when it comes to putting these tools into practice, these 6-point challenges will be very helpful in redefining your confidence.

These six-point challenges will be thoroughly covered. In addition, we will attempt to comprehend them from a factual standpoint rather than merely presenting them as some idealized, sugarcoated theories.

Challenge 1 – Begin with four good habits and establish a monthly goal to reach your objectives

This challenge is the simplest since it is the first step or initial level of a challenge. It's difficult to break a bad habit's pattern, but you can make new positive habits to start. I'll only suggest good practices here; you have to act quickly to identify the best. For reference, I'll give you a few brief examples, but ultimately, the choice is yours.

In order to understand how the positive habits listed below can change your life, let's look at a basic example of each habit.

Habits	Target per month	Results
Start reading	One book	Increased comprehension
Wake up early in the morning	70% success rate is must to achieve	Effective time management
Exercise without fail	80% of success rate (The goal is to walk 72 km in a month if you walk 3 km every day).	Better physical and mental health.
Help and support others	At least find one instance where you can offer your help.	Good vibes and genuine relationships.

The findings indicate that they are in line with our character and personality traits and will undoubtedly raise your PC score.

But while practicing these positive habits, one thing to remember is that we need to understand the distinction between targets and goals. Your target is the monthly threshold you set for yourself, and once you achieve your targets you move ahead to achieve your ultimate objective of reinventing yourself.

I've given you some examples of habits, but you are free to choose what suits you best. For instance, people who work in night shifts and are unable to wake up early, can adjust their routines accordingly. The basic idea is to use your effective time management skills. Anyone who is interested in helping others can perform a few small acts of charity without expecting any personal benefit, regardless of their income level.

To document your transformation journey, I have included a habit chart below.

Period	% target achieved for habit 1	% target achieved for habit 2	% target achieved for habit 3	% target achieved for habit 4	Average % target achieved for all habits
Month 1					
Month 2					
Month 3					
Month 4					
Month 5					
Month 6					
					Average of all six months

An example habit chart for your reference.

Period	Target % – Book reading 1/month	Target % – Waking up early Waking @ 5 AM	Target % – Exercise without fail Walk for 70 Km	Target % – Offer your help At least 1 person	Average % target achieved for all habits
Month 1	70	60	40	0	42.5
Month 2	80	70	50	100	75
Month 3	90	80	60	0	57.5
Month 4	80	80	50	0	52.5
Month 5	90	90	90	100	92.5
Month 6	100	90	90	100	95
The average of 6 months is 70 %					

You are headed in the right direction if your average target percentage is higher than 60%; if it is lower, you will need to re-evaluate your habits' charter.

Furthermore, you choose the targets as well, so you are the only one who can establish reasonable boundaries. You must therefore reevaluate your abilities at this point. Over the course of your six-month journey, you will progressively encounter numerous challenges. There's no need to worry if you're failing either, you just need to get back up and keep going until you reach your targets. This challenge cannot be abandoned. Only you will be able to advance to the next level of this difficult game once the level one is finished.

My experience leads me to recommend something that doesn't require much planning, stick to your daily goals and record your progress. You will feel stronger every day and have a higher percentage of hitting your goals. You will become so accustomed to your routine from this challenge that eventually, even if you want to cheat, your inner conscious mind will force you to meet your daily or weekly targets.

After six months, I'll wager once again that you would be a different person. At this point, you would also begin to sense TAMSO MA JYOTIRGAMAYA's essence.

Now is the moment for the second challenge level. ☺

Challenge 2 – Give up one bad habit

A bucket of water is filled with water to replace the air inside it. Our souls operate in a similar manner. Our behavior tends to be consistent regardless of what we think, do, or consume. A sportsperson you meet will always talk about diet, exercise routines, health issues, and fitness. A writer will constantly bring up new and original stories in their conversations. An entrepreneur will talk about new business concepts and how to attract investors if you meet them. A religious person you meet will talk about the positive aspects of their faith. Guys who are drug addicts will tell you how to get high and ignore this life cycle nonsense if you run into them. It's evident that knowing our habits helps us to achieve our goals and become the people we want to be and the same reflects into our conversations and behaviour.

I am not saying that you have to live a life filled with meaningless targets and goals, because that would make life too complex. However, living a life without purpose is akin to an animal's life, where its only purpose is to survive by finding food and shelter.

Though some might argue that they already practice many other good habits, like reading books, working out frequently, and keeping a low profile. Moreover, they simply want some quiet time to themselves and have no plans to achieve anything bigger in life. Even though you are acting kindly and without any lofty goals, you are inadvertently honing the qualities of your soul in this situation and are thus progressing along the path of soul exercise. Our goal in doing this exercise is to awaken the essence of our soul.

Funnier still, a lot of drug addicts say that they can also feel their soul whenever they get high. They touch their soul and feel it more profound, but that is just an illusion. Furthermore, this delusion is fleeting, as soon as they revert to their regular conscious state, the same agony returns. The good habits path is the right way to go if you're looking for a true soul experience that will last.

Let's go back to our second challenge, which is to give up one bad habit. You definitely want to naturally refrain from doing bad things. You can work on the second challenge more easily after you've finished the first.

Using a straightforward example, let's say someone has a junk food addiction. These people look for junk food joints wherever they go. When you're younger, it won't seem like a bad habit, but as you get older, it will start to affect you negatively. Not a single doctor on the planet would advise you to consume junk food. That's obviously a bad habit. However, after completing Challenge One, if an individual is deciding to lead a healthy lifestyle that includes regular exercise, the person's subconscious will start looking for nutritious foods and will discourage them from consuming junk food going forward.

I'm not saying that everything will magically happen in a month, but there will be a spark to stop going on any junk diets.

Let's look at one more complicated example, a highly successful man who is leading a wonderful life. In his field, he is a huge star and an inspiration to others. But he has a terrible smoking habit. Youngsters adore him and aspire to be just like him. This man is gifted with the soul, but he has a terrible habit that has held him back because of the way he has managed his life. Even though smoking is a bad habit, it doesn't define one's character, and influencing abilities are never easy to achieve. But due to his one bad habit, he may lose his credibility and can vanish his influencing power as well.

I had the opportunity to speak with a great deal of people, and the common response I heard from them all was that smoking makes them feel at ease and content.

Smoking allows them to have some alone time when they're feeling pressured by life and busy. It was clear from all of these talks that while each group of people is succeeding in their line of work, there is never enough time to connect with one's inner self. The fact that many of them were attempting to stop smoking but were unsuccessful.

I gave them a challenging but doable task to complete. I did not insist that they stop smoking, instead, I asked them to plant a tree every week. These guys did it gradually over several months. They used to take me along for the drive. They noticed that for the first few days after planting a tree, they used to smoke. They completed an excellent plantation in three to four months, and they knew a lot about how plants support this ecosystem. One of the guys made a joke one day while smoking and said "On one side, we talk about Oxygen and encourage people to come into this drive." On the other hand, this smoke is rotting our lungs". There was a pause for almost a minute. Suddenly, after something happens, the other guy says, "Let's end this right now." At least at this point, there was a strong sentiment regarding this bad habit and the reason it rose to the top due to the adoption of one excellent habit.

Additionally, we must comprehend how good and bad habits are mapped out. Since different people have different kinds of good and bad habits, you are the most knowledgeable person about your mapping as a vigilante.

What do I mean when I say mapping? Let's say you read great books and are an avid reader, but you're also a huge couch potato who spends all of your time in bed. You are doing well in one area, but you also need to make good use of your time. Therefore, you ought to be able to break your bad habit in these situations. Plan your challenges 1 and 2 in accordance with that.

Nobody will exist on this planet without any negative habits. You reexamine your introspection if you find none.

Let's say you are a fantastic writer and your books are well received by your readers. However, are you improving your writing or are you just writing because it feels right to you? Though it happens infrequently, intuition can be useful, which is why honing your writing technique is crucial. Reading the book for challenge one will take care of the problem, and embracing your errors and growing from them in challenge two will help you become a better writer.

Therefore, challenge 1 puts you on the correct track, and challenge 2 illuminates the path ahead by shutting a dark door in your life.

Let's now move to our next challenge.

Challenge 3 – Invest in you

Although I am referring to this in a financial sense, the term "investment" more accurately describes what we are doing here, which is investing in ourselves to produce valuable assets. Although human life is priceless, every individual has a personality and unique character. We behave in two distinct ways, and our decision-making processes are influenced by two factors: EQ and IQ.

Emotional quotient, or EQ, is a measure of our capacity for making emotional decisions and our inclination to behave in various emotionally charged scenarios. Conversely, IQ represents our intelligence quotient and defines us through the prism of rational conjecture. If we go farther, we will be able to communicate our choices with our hearts and minds. You become emotionally invested when you put your heart into something, and you make more rational, analytical decisions when you apply more of your intellect. Both are equally significant, and you can easily seize the appropriate opportunities if you are familiar with your quotients.

For instance, if you're a budding business owner aiming to launch your venture. The differentiators that set you and your company apart from the competition and provide you with a competitive advantage will be crucial components driving these setups. However, this needs to be done gradually; you need to devote all of your day and night to your passion and conduct extensive research. Study the appropriate material and skills. Obtain the necessary certifications so that when you join the market, people will be able to recognize your skills and place some trust in you.

When you invest into your own development and raises your EQ and IQ then you develop a trust quotient, or TQ. You are eligible for greater success the more trust you earn. Financial success is not the only thing I want to emphasize, when people begin to trust you, both personally and professionally, great things happen. Your influencing factor is also determined by your trust quotient; the more trust you have, the more influence you have over others.

As part of this challenge, set a goal for yourself to pursue particular courses and learning that will improve your professional, ethical, spiritual, or any other kind of learning that will help you become a more trustworthy person. That perimeter is yours to define.

Assume you are a craft artist who is just starting out in small business. People enjoy your creations, but you need assistance to grow. It implies that in order to make some financial deals, artists like you still need to build more trust. Now is the time to make an investment in yourself.

Learn about the craft market's paradigm and the latest trends in art. Recognize and pick up new skills, participate in workshops, and earn certifications. Disseminate all of these legitimate badges across your networks of contacts. You will experience a paradigm shift and have more options for financial gains when you take this action. We have to realize that improving your skills alone won't be enough to gain people's trust in this cutthroat society, hence, this exercise of self-investment and self-validation is a necessity.

That's why, the next time you get some spare earning, consider how you can use it to further your education, if that's not urgent, use it to purchase a fancy car. 😉

Challenge 4 – Digital fasting for 120 minutes /week

The practice of setting aside time for oneself from the outside world is known as digital fasting.

As we often say, there is no such thing as a silo in this globalized world. Therefore, I also want to be clear that this challenge is about giving you an opportunity to reflect on yourself rather than about cutting you off from this global family or making you work in silos.

We are all mostly motivated by outside forces. What will my partner's response be? How is my father going to respond? Does receiving good hikes require me to perform well?

All of these outside factors compel us to adopt a reactive mindset. Let's use an organization that operates in ABC nation as an example. In addition to abiding the laws and regulations of the nation in which the company operates, management will also take internal considerations into account, such as the kind of behavior, values, and organizational culture that the company must uphold. Therefore, for any established body, we always take both internal and external factors into account. However, when it comes to ourselves, we primarily consider external factors when making internal decisions.

Now let's go back to our challenge, we have to abstain from all digital networking devices for two hours every week.

Without a doubt, this challenge would be a difficult one. But let's examine and try to simplify this. Our daily target would be roughly 18 minutes since we want to reach our weekly target of 120 minutes. You are free to maintain this average and choose how to block out those eighteen minutes each day. If you already do any sort of meditations, then please make sure that this time is apart from your regular mediation hours.

What level of strictness would we need in this case? You would have to spend time away from all such things and devices that divert you from who you are, such as phones, computers, laptops, TVs, books, and social media.

Does that sound like a penalty? It's not, accepting yourself is the challenge here. You can think of anything good to talk about, and it would be nice to spend a few minutes with you.

Any emergency or pressing circumstance, though, will take precedence over this challenge.

I am aware that a lot of large companies have already adopted the policy of encouraging employees to avoid meetings and socializing on Fridays. The fundamental idea behind this is to spend quality time in your arena of expertise.

Why don't we choose to do this within our purview if it can be done professionally? We will gain some understanding of ourselves through this digital fast. Most people are unaware of their personality type, but by committing our favorite childhood memories, parent-child experiences, and friendship stories to memory, we can examine our character and determine what good or bad things we have done. You and your family can talk about these matters. You can converse with your family members during a digital fast, but you are prevented from using electronic devices.

Same as of previous challenges, you are responsible for scheduling these daily 15 to 20 minutes of digital fasting and choosing how you want to spend this valuable time.

Since these gadgets are similar to addictions and we wouldn't be able to kick them out as quickly, hence, don't lose hope if you can't finish these fasting minutes during your first few days of the challenge. Furthermore, they play a crucial role in your life. Nonetheless, it would be best to decide on your priorities.

If, for example, your phone rings in the middle of your digital fasting, you won't be able to answer it and will therefore miss it. You can gradually let your friends, closed group, distant families, coworkers and superiors know that during this window of time, you won't be able to take any calls and that they should wait for your call back. It's perfectly acceptable to share this explanation. Yes, isn't always preferable to no. Saying no to people with grace is a skill that we should all acquire.

But let's consider one more scenario, let's say an unanticipated emergency arises during your fasting hours. Since you won't be able to contact anyone, keep a backup emergency number and a list of people who can act in your place and notify you of any updates via other channels so that you are aware of the situation as soon as possible. The majority of us are prepared for these scenarios and have backup plans in place. Furthermore, as we said previously too these scenarios will take precedence over our challenge because they are the most important and unlikely to occur.

Challenge 5 – A complete day of financial fasting once a month

We took a break from this digital world in the last challenge. We now need to consider our financial situation. Determine whether you are controlling your money cycle or being driven by materialistic things in this fast-paced world where people are chasing comfort and a lucrative lifestyle. We are all aware that material happiness exists and can occasionally be very important. But we don't really need as many of the items we usually purchase.

Although I do not support living frugally, think about this: if you spend $100 a day, what are the values you bring into your life.

If you want to purchase a high-quality vehicle and your budget permits you to purchase a luxury vehicle, then by all means do so, but, anticipate your financial forecasts carefully and decide. When it comes to comfort, luxury cars are excellent. These shouldn't, however, just be purchased for show or to garner fictitious respect, doing so could lead to more serious problems in the future.

That implies that the task is to spend no money at all for at least one day out of each month. This will enable you to track your spending habits and guarantee that you create a more effective financial plan for your family and yourself. Being unable to remember a day in the last few years when you haven't spent any money means that this challenge will likely become more difficult. This is a true statement for all income brackets

Being able to shop from home in this digital age is a great advancement for society and has benefited a lot of people who are unable or unwilling to visit physical marketplaces. But because branding is so profitable and the economy is expanding, shopping features are turning into an addiction. One may argue that since many people struggle to make ends meet, it is impossible for them to afford to spend money on such addictive shopping.

This argument is sound, but the habit of unnecessary spending is a distinguishing characteristic that extends into all income groups with varying scales and magnitudes. Hence, this is a challenge that anyone from any income bracket can take up, and a one-day fast won't have a big effect on economy. But as I've previously stated, any emergency will always take precedence over our challenges, so be sure to abide by that general guideline.

This challenge will eventually pay off in the form of significant economic stability. But once your financial fast is over, you should keep an eye on your spending habits. If you suddenly increase your spending, your fast will be ineffective.

This task will instill in you the values of high thinking and simple living in addition to financial resonance. There is no bypass or substitute because this fasting is not intended to adhere to any traditions or routines.

Challenge 6 – Community excellence day once a month

This challenge is not like any of the others, while the previous five challenges have all focused on becoming independent, this one will teach us how to achieve optimal interdependence.

You are mistaken if you believe that your personality type, extroverted or introverted, will have any bearing on this challenge. Instead of emphasizing making lots of connections, it is about using your resources, money, time, and skills to support the community and society.

To put it another way, let's say you're a superb attorney with a stellar reputation in your community. Choose a day when you can use your expertise to assist a client who is unable to pay for your services. If you decide to take on this work on your own, the amount of time you want to spend is up to you, so adjust your time management accordingly. You shouldn't feel overburdened by this task, nor should it go beyond your regular obligations. If you are a medical professional, set aside some time to assist and treat those in need within the scope of your work.

The main task at hand is figuring out how to best assist people without considering the personal gains.

It will now be questioned how others who are not involved in community services can contribute here, after all, both of these examples come from organizations that provide community services, which already gives them a greater opportunity to benefit society.

Suppose, you are a talented writer who publishes books, so you can still handle this in your capacity. To impart your expertise on how to write a captivating book, you could host some workshops. If you're an actor or artist, consider how you can best brand any social cause with your name. If you're a stay-at-home mom, consider cooking some food for the local orphanages or other community organizations that provide food to the less fortunate.

Some people may argue that they are already practicing this challenge because they regularly donate to charities. Giving money to a charity doesn't mean you've accomplished service excellence, charity is one of the subsets of community service. The goal of this challenge is to use your time, abilities, principles, and efforts to help others and obtain mutual positivity rather than to just donate something.

Serving people and societies is just one aspect of service excellence; you can also use this to benefit the environment. It is also Mother Nature's reflection, on this challenge. Natural resources are self-giving and never ask for anything in return. Overexploitation causes it to self-correct, that's why we refer to it as a natural disaster. Given how much we take from nature and how much we must give back, we must therefore live in harmony with it.

I've provided numerous examples to help make the challenge's request simpler. Once again, though, the kind of service you select is entirely up to you. To finish this challenge, we have to guarantee one such day per month. Please make your assessment appropriately if you are taking on any such community service that will require a lot of work. It should be doable for you, as I previously stated. The service excellence assignment needs to fit into what you can do right now.

You may experience some awkwardness in the beginning of this challenge, and your shyness and social ego may cause some difficulties. However, get rid of this feeling as soon as possible to begin your wonderful journey. You don't have to worry about what others will think of you or how your family will respond when you start your challenge. Please talk about this with your elders and family and seek their advice, but be sure to plan this challenge with clarity.

Despite the many challenges ahead, it seems certain that you will find enjoyment in your journey of challenge. But if you stick with this practice, I promise that after six months your life will have completely changed and transformed. You will definitely have a PC score of 2 from now on, and your life will resemble picture 4 from chapter 1.

Let's examine how the following traits will be achieved using this challenge framework:

Personal Growth and Development:

- Starting a Good Habit: Introducing positive habits into your routine can contribute to personal growth and development.
- Stopping a Bad Habit: Eliminating a negative behavior can lead to personal improvement and better mental and physical well-being.

Self-Reflection and Awareness:

- Investing in Yourself: Taking time and resources to invest in your skills, knowledge, and overall well-being promotes self-awareness and a deeper understanding of your capabilities.

Mindful Technology Use:

- Digital Fasting: Temporarily disconnecting from digital devices and social media helps in reducing stress, improving focus, and fostering real-world connections. It can contribute to better mental health.

Financial Well-Being:

- Financial Fasting: Going on a spending hiatus or being more mindful of your expenses can lead to better financial management, savings, and a reduced financial burden.

Building Discipline:

- Challenges in Habit Formation: Initiating and maintaining positive changes, whether in habits or finances, requires discipline. These challenges can instill a sense of self-discipline that can be applied in various aspects of life.

Community Engagement:

- Community Service Day: Participating in community service fosters a sense of social responsibility and empathy. It can create a positive impact on both the community and the individual, enhancing a sense of purpose and fulfillment.

Improved Mental Health:

- Balancing Habits: Combining positive habits, mindfulness, and community engagement can contribute to improved mental health. Physical activity, social connections, and personal growth are all factors that positively influence mental well-being.

Sense of Achievement:

- Completing Challenges: Successfully completing these challenges provides a sense of accomplishment and boosts self-esteem. It reinforces the idea that change is possible with commitment and effort.

Stress Reduction:

- Mindful Practices: Whether through digital fasting or community service, these challenges can help reduce stress by providing moments of relaxation, connection, and purpose.

Healthy Lifestyle:

- Overall Well-Being: The combination of positive habits, financial mindfulness, and community engagement contributes to a holistic approach to health and well-being.

- Remember that the effectiveness of these challenges may vary from person to person, and it's important to approach them with realistic expectations and a willingness to adapt as needed.

We must make sure that, despite our transformation, we continue to have significance for both this society and for ourselves. Why is this meaningfulness necessary? We will talk about this in our upcoming chapter.

Meaningfulness vs Usefulness

There are two main categories of ideology that persist in our society.

Accuse authority and build your kingdom, advises one ideology. The rest of the population has to adopt the same. If you look closely, this reflects the global market ideology that is currently dominant in our world. Before we have money or the power to take over the entire world, we have many benefits, honor, and importance. Once our power is taken away, we won't be treated the same way.

Another ideology seeks power, money, and significance but does not base its relevance on having friends with advantages. Rather than being advantageous, the foundation of this ideology is to become meaningful. People are therefore treated like a large family in the domain of this ideology. Everybody in their domain is taken care of by the leader in this system.

Spiritual books written in Hinduism tell a well-known tale. These two ideologies had a hard time making an impression when power poles first started to emerge. **Vilochan** was the founder of a philosophy that valued strength and utility. An ideology centered on meaningfulness was led by **Indra**. One day, they got into a heated argument over which ideology was superior. Finally, they both decided to see Brahma, the universe's creator.

When they arrived at Brahma's place, they both saw that he was occupied with creating this beautiful nature elements for the benefit of this lovely world. They bided their time until Brahma completed his necessary duties. When Brahma eventually joined them, he inquired as to why they had come to his place. Vilochan gave his explanation for visiting and requested his insightful counsel.

We already learned in the last chapter on "Science of Actions" that while humans have no control over the outcomes of their actions, they can control their thoughts and emotions, which in turn shapes their behavior.

Thus, it was evident to Brahma as well. These two power poles were also created by Brahma, but he also gave humans the ability to choose their own ideologies, lifestyles, and actions in the world.

He questioned Indra. "I recognized that you both adhere to your own ideologies, and I have no right to judge which of you is superior. However, if you have any logical questions, I can assist you in answering them.

Vilochan and Indra were irritated because their creator was downplaying their importance and value. Together, they had a discussion and asked another question.

"May I know if I could see my soul and control my results, too?" inquired Vilochan.

Brahma gestured for Indra to follow suit and ask the same question.

With a nod, Indra agreed to this question.

The universe's creator, Brahma, attempted to solve this using logic, so instead of giving them the solution up front, he gave them an assignment to complete and promised to reveal their soul and grant the control over their own destiny if they passed.

Brahma went on to say that you had to look each other in the eyes and tell me who you saw.

It was easy to figure out: mirror reflection allowed both of them to see each other in their eyes. Still, perception is altered here by intelligence and long-term vision. Due to his tendency toward self-centeredness and his belief in his world of power, Vilochan asserted that he could see his soul in everything, seeing himself reflected in the beauty of the natural world. Thanking Brahma for enlightening him, he expressed gratitude for being able to control this nature and become the omnipresent superpower.

On the other side, Indra had a different perception. He also saw himself in Vilochan's eyes and everywhere in this nature. He realized that he should take care of this nature because nature is an integral part of his life, and his existence is due to this beautiful nature. He requested Brahma to make him a guard of this nature so that he could save humanity and life in this universe.

The rest is history as it is. Vilochan rose to become the world's most powerful natural ruler, and Indra became the monarch of all the gods of nature. In the end, both possessed powers, but their goals were distinct.

However, the Kingdom of Vilochan ultimately came to an end when a more powerful person acquired both the Kingdom and his power. On the other hand, Indra continued to be significant and is still relevant today because of his integrity toward nature.

In addition, we should aim to live more meaningful lives rather than merely being functional. You can be valuable in your workplace or in your line of work, but meaningful work will ensure that your growth is long-lasting.

Let's use examples from our everyday lives to better understand what it means to be meaningful and useful.

Mr. Sharma held a prominent role in a reputable organization and was worthy of a promotion in recognition of his well-received contributions. His level of focus was so great that he was able to show off very creative abilities in his line of work. He was able to effectively manage his family at the same time. He was a prolific author who wrote numerous books on the gains and profits of business.

His boss abruptly asked him to leave the company during the 2008 recession, citing the company's negative growth and inability to compete in the market. The top management had made the decision to eliminate some positions with higher compensation. Mr. Sharma was one of those unfortunate individuals.

He felt depressed and angry to hear this news. He asked his supervisor how he could be fired when he had devoted his entire life to this company and everything he had done was used as a case study for students to learn from.

Being open with him, his boss showed him the top leadership letter outlining their plans to implement innovative market approaches and develop a new brand. Since Mr. Sharma was more interested in and knowledgeable about physical market presence, his position in this new strategy was becoming less and less relevant.

Following 2008, companies realized the value of global online marketplaces that allowed them to rapidly establish connections with customers anywhere in the world.

Even so, Mr. Sharma had implemented a number of noteworthy strategies and efforts to boost sales in physical markets. His efforts were not relevant to the company.

We can readily understand from this example that we will gain until the point at which we are no longer useful, but after that point, we will become irrelevant. As a result, it is imperative that we always consider our significance.

We can use the music industry as another example. Beat-based music is always less impactful than songs with strong and meaningful lyrics. Long term, lyrics-based songs will be remembered while beat-based music may draw in more listeners and become a chartbuster in the short term.

The same holds true for our lives and lessons learned. Remember that the quest for significance and meaning is a personal and ongoing journey. It involves continuous self-discovery and a willingness to adapt and grow. Be patient with yourself and celebrate the small victories along the way.

If you use our frameworks for the Five Rules and Challenges, you will become more meaningful than just useful.

Realizing that these practices must continue is also crucial. Therefore, let's read about how to carry on with these practices in the upcoming chapter.

R-R-R Rule of Life

Every single person in the entire universe is convinced of the good things in life. We also learned in the last few chapters how to reinvent our inner selves in order to bring positivity into our lives. The basic tenet of life is love, but it's not the love between lovers; rather, it's the love of your inner self. We can see the various facets of life when we begin to love who we are.

We can expand the definition of "life" as follows if we can determine what the greatest meaning of life is.

L – LIVE

I – IT

F – FOR

E – EVER

There is no secret when we say "live forever," but simply breathing is not a formula for living; rather, we can say that we are living life to the fullest when we are in harmony with our inner selves and experience no inner conflicts.

Let's understand this with a simple example –

When your spouse wants to visit a beach, but you are planning a trip to a hilly location, how do you decide which is better and know when you are not at odds with your soul?

There might be two cases:

- Case 1 – Even though you'd rather visit the mountains, you also value your relationship, so you choose to go to the beaches in order to make your spouse happy. In this instance, you are in harmony with your soul because you have an enduring love or concern for your partner. We also receive the same amount of respect when we do this.

- Case 2 – You choose to have a clear conversation with your spouse about your issue because you detest beaches and are unable to spend even a moment there. Now, in this instance, circumstances might be different –
    - Situation 1 – Your partner chooses to visit the mountains after acknowledging your worries. No problems and joyful times.
    - Situation 2 – Your partner is inflexible and does not respect your decisions; they do not wish to have them changed. In this instance, the conflict is not just internal to you but also external to your relationships.

In situation 2, happy moments are mostly transformed into terrible actions and differences are made.

It's also safe to say that disagreements of this kind happen occasionally, so we need to learn how to resolve conflicts. We won't preach here; that is for your conscience, but if you are feeling frustrated or having an angry outburst, please don't hesitate to contact your support system. However, try reaching out to your inner self during this outburst as well to get some guidance.

We gained a lot of knowledge about the PC framework, Rules & Challenges Framework, and the Karma theory, but maintaining this inner soul connection is not always easy. You will experience a diversion as soon as it is disconnected.

The question that now arises is. How can we maintain a connection with ourselves? It's not simple, as I mentioned, but it's also not unachievable.

An RRR formula exists that can assist us in establishing a perfect connection.

R-R-R stands for Recognize, Respect, and Recall.

When embarking on a new journey, the RRR rule is helpful and should be followed. If you look closely, you'll see that everything in nature follows this very natural rule.

The R-R-R is also followed when we pray every day.

We acknowledge the Almighty's power, show him the utmost respect, and let go of all our egos before Him. As a result, we constantly adhere to the first two R&R.

Next, R is tricky. We all know that GOD is the world's creator, that is universally accepted in all the religions, so why do we recall the proven fact?

Thus, the question of what precisely needs to be recalled arises.

God's power is not something we need to remember. But to attain that degree of purity with God, we must recall the human practices.

This also holds true for our rules and challenges framework. We are all aware of how beneficial these are in helping everyone stay on the correct path. Everyone can follow the first two Rs because they are simple to understand, but the third R informs us that remembering and continuing the practices will improve our lives.

Let us get some more details about these RRR rules.

Recognize – We would need to assess our strengths and weaknesses first. We all possess both of these things. You can also do that introspection with the assistance of the earlier chapters in this book. Therefore, the first step is realizing who you are.

I will state that in this instance, caution is necessary. Because rational trust requires us to act in accordance with our abilities and preferences, hence. first R is important.

It would be a waste of time to go and start learning how to sing if you are not a good singer. You can study singing theory, but you'll never be a proficient vocalist. Thus, logical trust informs us, what we can achieve, and what is mapped to our capabilities.

Respect – Respect your inner conscience and your abilities, advises Second R. When you have reasonable confidence in yourself, only you can positively evolve. You are capable of anything if you have self-confidence. Because we don't believe in our abilities, we frequently fail to start good things.

Recall – Though it comes last, as we have learned, memory is important. When we take an exam, we always remember the courses that we have read or learned in class. Likewise, we need to constantly remind ourselves of excellent habits, insightful readings, and encouraging ideas.

As we've seen in the previous chapters, our definition of what is good or bad is subjective and will not be predetermined. Everything we have read in the earlier chapters is simple to understand the first time around, but we won't benefit from it until we put it into practice frequently. Humans are the most intelligent species on Earth, and its common knowledge that we all have both positive and negative energy. Which one we need to use to dominate is now up to us.

Embracing Gratitude: A Heartfelt Acknowledgment to Our Transformative Journey Together

This heartfelt acknowledgment extends beyond mere words, I hope this book has given you the insight of your own life's shared experiences, challenges, and triumphs that have woven your path of success. This was a small attempt on my part to impart the experience I've gained over the past few years. As you have also read in the book, there are no short cuts to success, and if we go beyond our life's stress and grow into more meaningful individuals, then success is guaranteed and we will also make a big impact in our field of endeavor.

As you have turned the pages, you have come to appreciate the beauty of recognizing not just the high points but also the low points of your journey, realizing that each turn has added richness to the fabric of your lives.

Finally, I want to express my gratitude to each and every one of you for coming along on this life-changing adventure. I hope you have found this to be an engaging and meaningful experience. I request to encourage you to recognize and appreciate your accomplishments. Acknowledge the progress that has been made and convey hope for each person's journey to continue evolving.

Since our main goal is to change and make our lives more meaningful, you can consult other reliable sources as well to make sure you are receiving the most recent information to refer to and act upon. I'll also try to share more information in my capacity to spread this knowledge as well.

I would like to reiterate that there are always fresh opportunities for growth and discovery, and that the transformative journey is never-ending for all us and will always be relevant. Let's continue in this transformative exploration, where gratitude becomes the compass guiding us toward a future filled with meaning, connection, and a profound appreciation for the journey we've traveled together.

In the last, I would love to hear many more such motivational tales from all of you. Please also don't hesitate to share with your trusted circle if you see any benefits and feel free to get in touch and work with us to make this journey more inclusive.